D1236784

Foreign Travelers in America
1810–1935

Foreign Travelers in America
1810–1935

Advisory Editors:

Arthur M. Schlesinger, Jr.
Eugene P. Moehring

MIDAS

OR

The United States and the Future

C. H. BRETHERTON

ARNO PRESS
A New York Times Company
New York—1974

Reprint Edition 1974 by Arno Press Inc.

Reprinted from a copy in
  The Newark Public Library

FOREIGN TRAVELERS IN AMERICA, 1810-1935
ISBN for complete set: 0-405-05440-8
See last pages of this volume for titles.

Manufactured in the United States of America

Library of Congress Cataloging in Publication Data

Bretherton, Cyril Herbert Emmanuel, 1878 or 9-1939.
  Midas; or, The United States and the future.

  (Foreign travelers in America, 1810-1935)
  Reprint of the 1926 ed. published by Kegan Paul,
Trench, Trubner, London, in series: To-day and to-
morrow.
  1. United Satates--Civilization--20th century.
I. Title. II. Title. The United States and the
future. III. Series. IV. Series: To-day and to-
morrow.
E169.B83 1974   917.3'03'91   73-13123
ISBN 0-405-05445-9

MIDAS
OR THE
UNITED STATES AND THE FUTURE

TO-DAY AND TO-MORROW

*A full List of this Series
will be found at the end
of this Volume*

MIDAS

OR

The United States and the Future

BY

C. H. BRETHERTON

LONDON
KEGAN PAUL, TRENCH, TRUBNER & CO., Ltd.
New York: E. P. DUTTON & CO.
1926

Made and Printed in Great Britain by
M. F. Robinson & Co., Ltd., at The Library Press Lowestoft

CONTENTS

PREFACE

I lived too long in the United States to be able to reproduce any of those " first fine careless raptures " that make the literary Englishman's fleeting impressions of the United States such excellent reading. To compensate for a certain lack of sprightliness I have conjured up a vision of the United States of the future whose fabric is based on such substantial if not always inspiring matters as history, geography and political economy. Solid bodies notoriously resist compression and two whole chapters, one on the International Future and the other on the Industrial Future of the United States have been jettisoned to keep the column to the requisite length. The former subject, embracing, as it does, the future of Canada, may well be allotted a volume of its own. The Industrial future of the United States is dealt with as well as may be in the Conclusion.

Some time ago I read in a little volume of poems one by a lady called *Hates*. It recounted the various things the authoress disliked and contains the following lines :

> " I hate washing dirty plates.
> I hate the United States."

Those who hate the United States will get no satisfaction out of this volume. They will much prefer *Babbit*, and *Main Street*. Enthusiasts for the world's biggest republic will hardly be more satisfied but I do not know what antidote to recommend them unless it be the *Saturday Evening Post*.

C.H.B.

Boar's Hill,
Oxford, January, 1926.

MIDAS

OR THE

FUTURE OF THE UNITED STATES

INTRODUCTION

The incident of the Tower of Babel has never been rightly understood nor its valuable lesson appreciated. Ill fares the land to hastening ills a prey when contractors accumulate and lexicographers decay. The greatest single obstacle in the path of Civilization has been the fact that no two people ever attach precisely the same meaning to the same word. Science, by proclaiming that nothing is or can be stationary or positive or incapable of further analysis, is responsible for this undesirable state of affairs. Fundamentalism is a belated revolt against it. America is preparing to make war on the Oxford English Dictionary. A mediaeval English scholar propounded the monstrous fallacy that writing maketh an exact man. Tennessee denies it. Writing, it claims, may once have been a reliable means of expressing ideas.

It has become a merely haphazard method of provoking opinions. Language is so full of buts and wells that the task of finding truth at the bottom of any one of them is well nigh hopeless.

The remedy is obvious. You cannot abolish language. The poets and praise-makers of earth are irrepressible. The spellbinders are intrenched behind their box office receipts. The saints and sages who discuss of this and that so wisely are quite accustomed to having their mouths filled with dust. You cannot abolish language which, however inconvenient, has its uses. You can abolish Truth which cannot be proved to be of the slightest use to anybody.

" Civilization " is one of the terms that are easily used but difficult to define. The Babelonian who invented it had reason to be proud of his devastating handiwork. It involves the fundamental idea of law, not law in conduct only, but law in thought and in taste, not law on the statute book only but law in the minds of men. The jurisprudents have sufficiently analysed the relation of concrete law to civilization. Not the number or excellence of a country's laws but the extent to which they are obeyed is the real test of its civilization. In the last ten years the United States have passed over five hundred thousand legislative enactments. In the same period Great Britain passed seventeen thousand. At the same time fifty murders are committed in the United States to every one committed in Great Britain. Obedience to law is not the sole test. It must be a voluntary obedience finding its inspiration in the popular will. In Mexico under the Diaz regime there was remarkably little crime, but this was due not to respect of the law but to fear of those charged with its enforcement. The same was true in a lesser degree in regard to Ireland and Russia.

Theoretical anarchists push this argument further and maintain that if men kept steadily before them the ideal of no law instead of the ideal of more law or better law a Civilization could be evolved--the highest known—in which there would be no law. It is a fallacious argument because all that would happen would be that convention would replace written law, The code of behaviour would remain though the sanctions might disappear. A really lawless condition—the game of communal life played without any rules at all—cannot even be imagined. For where Civilization, as opposed to abstract morality, is concerned regulative law is even more important than moral law ; the *mala prohibita* are more disastrous to the community life than the *mala in se.*

The explanation is obvious. Moral codes are as often founded on taste and accident as on necessity or convenience. Regulative laws have a strictly utilitarian basis. If the people of Manchester or Peoria suddenly decided to set all the moral laws at defiance some confusion would ensue (though the result might not be as disastrous as some would wish us to believe) but it would not be comparable in its catastrophic consequencies to a sudden decision of the people to throw all their refuse into the street instead of putting it in garbage cans and ash barrels for removal by the local authorities.

We may even go further and say that from the point of view of comparative civilization the nature and quality of moral law is totally irrelevant. A country which has marriage but no divorce is not more likely to be civilized than one which does not recognise marriage as a legal status. A community which feeds its superfluous female children to the crocodiles from utilitarian motives is not necessarily inferior in civilization to one that allows them to grow up and draw the dole. There are, indeed, certain moral offences which seem at first sight to be intolerable under any circumstances —murder, for example, and theft—but on analysis it will be found in every case that it is only for regulative purposes that their prohibition becomes essential. When duelling was popular and permissible a skilful swordsman could murder any tyro he chose to dislike with impunity. All the public demanded was that the killing should be done with decorum in an inconspicuous spot and that there should be no brawling in frequented places.

Put the thing in another way. A moral code is a collection of utilitarian rules that time or circumstance has invested with a sentimental value. The utilitarian value may have wholly or partially disappeared. It does not matter unless the obsolete rule is retained in the legal as well as the moral code. The moral code still requires us to tell the truth on all occasions. Such a course no longer has any material value though we may pursue it as a matter of sentiment. The law however no longer compels us to tell the truth except under certain very restricted circumstances. Unlike the moral code it is up-to-date.

A people is most likely to be civilized if its legal clothes are a good fit. If it has grown out of them or if, in a spirit of intemperate optimism it has had them made several sizes too large it will show an increasing tendency to leave them off except on state occasions. The children in Southern Ireland take their boots off to walk to school and put them on to sit in class. A people whose laws are too fine for every day use will act in a similar manner. It follows that a full gaol is generally a sign not that there are a lot of bad men about, but a lot of bad laws.

When we talk of the future of the United States we necessarily mean the degree and kind of civilization that it is likely in the future to evolve. We cannot speculate on this without calling some or all of these general considerations to aid. But Civilization involves much besides the law of conduct. There are laws of the mind to be considered. Without them there can be no standards of taste, no aesthetic values. Here we are on difficult ground. Is beauty constant and fundamental or subject to the varying influences of custom and sentiment? Does utility besides stimulating art subconsciously mould taste? We need not attempt to go deeply into these and similar questions. If the national life is vigorous and individual the spiritual and aesthetic life will be equally robust. Law, itself susceptible of vigorous growth, will be present in either case.

Conduct and culture are the main criteria by which the comparative civilization of a people are assessed but they are not the only ones. A community may have wise and well respected laws and a vigorous aesthetic life and yet its religion may be unenlightened, its education restricted, its economic system unsound, its political machinery antiquated and unwieldy. Virginia in the slavery days was more civilized, comparatively, than any of the United Staes are to-day. Switzerland has good laws, good education, a strong economic position, a healthy religious life and an admirable constitution but its contributions to learning and the arts are negligible. All these aspects of the national life must be considered by the writer of such a book as this but with pronounced caution for they are all subjects of contention among the learned and the divine. To the honest biologist all religion is unenlightened. To the consistent Tory education is a calamity and there is still much to be said for an enlightened system of slavery. The Socialist can see nothing good in the capitalistic system and the competing claims to pre-eminence of republics, autocracies and limited monarchies, of elastic and rigid constitutions, of representation and delegation, of direct primaries and proportional representation and the other panaceas that the political flesh is a prey to are all tried subjects of more or less heated debate.

We are subject to a further limitation. Civilization is comparative. There is no definite line which marks, as it were, the desert from the sown. The Greeks who liked definition called all other races but themselves " barbarians " indiscriminately. Most nations still regard this as the handiest working classification, but nowadays modesty prevents us from saying so. Moreover the peoples that have loudest proclaimed themselves the sole repositories of culture and custodians of the authentic wellsprings of civilization have always got into trouble by it. In any case it is clear that the careful analysis that the scientific student will make in weighing this civilization and that is a very different thing from the haphazard comparisons that suggest themselves to the layman.

The subject is capable of infinite subdivision and enlargement, it has a hundred facets and can be examined from a thousand angles. This cannot be done in a hundred pages which is perhaps just as well. Our business is to get a good view of the wood, not to examine the trees. We must avoid the trivial and yet ignore none of the tremendous trifles that inform the moving scene with distinction and individuality. Take for example, such an apparently trifling thing as cold pumpkin pie. You would say that such a little thing could not possibly have any material bearing on the present or future civilisation of a great people. You would be wrong. The American pie—a thin layer of squashed fruit between two slabs of underdone dough—is a dietetic bomb. Chaperoned by unlimited draughts of iced water it is the father and mother of the galloping dyspepsia that afflicts to a greater or less degree three out of every five Americans. This dyspepsia has already done more to mould the temper and habits of the people of the United States than Puritanism, the Pioneer spirit, Christian Science, slavery and the Irish politician all rolled into one. It is the prime cause of American divorce. It is the greatest single factor in the moulding of American speech. It affects (adversely) American thought. For a reflective and philosophical mind can only be maintained in the presence of a good digestion, while the drilling of action driven thought into the rock face of material things acts as a counter irritant. Dyspepsia is even the dominating factor in the moulding of the new American Physiognomy, having already ousted from pride of place in this respect the great American Catarrh which gave New England its prototypes of the conventional cartoonist's Uncle Sam.

Influences of this kind are necessarily transient but their results remain. Already an eupeptic American, immune to ice water and pie, and capable of assimilating

any quantity cold storage food without
any ill effects, is being evolved. Neverthe-
less he still carries upon him the traces
of his dyspeptic ancestry. Cold pie has
set its mark upon the race. And so have
and will many other things apparently
of no account. For it is things and not
ideas that mould the destinies of men and
races though man, who is much more
concerned with what he thinks than with
what he makes, refuses to recognize it.
This is particularly true of a country
like the United States which has behind
it no long and complicated history whose
lesson—the invariable lesson of history—
is that when ideas begin to dominate
disaster generally follows and that it is
better to let things have it their own way
or, as we say, to let nature take its course.
A single example may suffice. Alcohol
is a thing. Prohibition is an idea. Alcohol
has played an immense part in the moulding of civilization and will always do so
because it is there and must be reckoned
with. Prohibition has yet to make its
mark. It has made a little history—if we
assume that the power of Islam is in part
attributable to it—but it has contributed
nothing to civilization. The people of
the United States have still a lot to go
through before they learn to recognize
that notions cannot be substituted for
facts. To-day they are largely engaged in

attempting definitely to substitute what they would like to be and what they like to think for what is, not as we do in the old world, as a piece of happy but rather pathetic make-believe but with the aid of bell, book, and candle, the statute thereunto appertaining and the Ku Klux Klan. A question arises which must be answered here. Why, it may be asked, should we suppose that there will ever be an identifiably American civilization ? What reason is there for assuming that in fifty or a hundred years from now the United States will not be doing very much what it is, doing to-day, that is to say leading Europe in the production and accumulation of wealth and tagging along behind as a comparatively indifferent exponent of European culture ? Could this question not be satisfactorily answered there would obviously be very little excuse for writing this book whose purpose is far less to draw a picture of the United States as they will appear at some future date as to demonstrate why and how they are diverging from the channels in which our European civilization flows into others that are or will be exclusively their own. The American people quite obviously have a future and a material civilization that is bound to develop in remarkable ways. This has to be considered but no great interest

would attach to the business if we did
not feel entitled to assume that on this
material civilization is to be founded
an intellectual civilization highly developed, boldly individual in character and
having a great if not a predominating
influence on world culture generally.
We can discuss the United States of fifty
or a hundred years hence in terms of
population, industries, agriculture,
military and naval power, territorial
expansion and actual and potential wealth,
possibly with astonishment or even alarm
but with reasonable certainty. With less
assurance but with greater interest we
can discuss them in terms of poetry and
painting, of music and architecture, of laws
and customs and morals and manners, of
tastes and habits and beliefs. The proof
of the pudding in this case will be the
eating. It is the business of this book
to prove (if that is necessary) that an
American civilization is coming by indica-
ting the directions in which and the conditions under which it is already
developing.

It is often alleged that there can only
be one civilization though there can be
many phases of it and many national or
racial or periodic contributions to it.
The point is unimportant. We talk of
Egyptian and Greek, and Roman and
Chinese civilizations and know quite

well what we mean, namely that Egypt and Greece and Rome and Japan have made contributions to civilization so numerous, so original and so coherent in point of time that we are compelled to consider them as a whole. In that sense we propose to discuss the future civilization of the United States. It may be that they will not develop any new attribute of civilization, any new art or new field of intellectual activity. We cannot rule out that possibility because Science forbids us to assume that any further expansion of man's intellectual activity must be one of degree and not of kind, or that the machine man of 1925 has before him an evolutionary horizon less extensive than that which lay before the ape man of 20,000 B.C. Centuries, however, if not thousands of years, have elapsed since a new art was discovered. The explanation is not that the limits set to art by the senses and the mind together have everywhere been reached, but that the things with which the face of civilization has been changed in that time, steam and steel and electricity and high explosives and the products of commercial chemistry, have not offered, or have not been called upon to offer, any scope for the inspirations of creative art.

Men did not look to art to create its own opportunities, but when utility had

been satisfied it was the custom of art
to step in. To-day that custom is in
desuetude. We have only to consider
the motor car. Here was a new medium
for artistic expression if ever there was
one, but the automobile remains a machine,
with as little claim to aesthetic distinction
as the spinning jenny or the Hoe press.
This may be, as far as Europe is concerned
at least, because we have acquired our
new scientific civilization too quickly
to be quite at home with it. Accepting
the ant-heap life because we have not the
courage, like Samuel Butler's Erewhonians,
to smash the machines and knock the
inventors and scientists on the head,
we remain sentimentally and aesthetically
attached to the past, and to such old and
tried things as gave art its impulses when
civilization was at its dawn. If we venture
to think that it will be the Americans
who first begin to give real artistic expression to the machine-run, gadget-studded,
power-controlled civilization-by-numbers
to which the modern world seems hope-
lessly committed, it is not because we
think they are more informed with
spiritual vigour, but because the new
conditions are moulded nearer to their
hearts' desire than to that of the European,
because they have already acquired or
are about to acquire the outlook and

temper and habit of mind of the machine age.

It is significant, in this connection, that the United States has already contributed to civilization the only two new art forms that have appeared in a century. It may be a painful thought but it is the fact that to-day the hand that rocks Tin Pan Alley rules the musical world. And King Jazz was born and founded his original kingdom in the United States because his restless, exciting and superficial cacophonies are a true expression of the spirit of the American people and the pace and gait of American life. The other contribution is the skyscraper, architecturally still in its infancy, but as full of possibilities as the old architectural forms are, in modern hands and for modern purposes, full of emptiness. Let those who doubt this go and feast their eyes on the new Regent Street. Aesthetically it is a smudge. It lacks all the quiet dignity of the old Regent Street—naturally, since modern business is neither quiet nor dignified—but it also lacks the assertion of commercial power, the sheer, efficient majesty of the skyscraper. The new Regent Street is a meaningless compromise, not because British architecture is at a low ebb, but because British commerce and industry are in a bad way;

because British business is to-day in a transitional stage, endeavouring (with no great success) to compromise between the dignified three-story-and-basement operations of the Victorian epoch and the fifty story, steel-frame methods of the American commercial octopus.

The new commercial civilization seems destined to swallow up Europe and Tin Pan Alley is the war drum of the new (American) white man round the world. As its spirit goes marching on, and an intellectual civilization to match begins to take shape and evolve and spread, it is the American who will lead and the European who, with many a backward glance at the good old days, will tag along behind.

Chapter I

THE FUTURE OF THE
MELTING POT

The present population of the United
States is somewhere in the neighbourhood
of 110,000,000 or about thirty-five to
the square mile. One or two of the Eastern
States, notably Massachusetts, Rhode
Island and New Jersey, have already
reached a maximum density of population.
Others such as Arizona, New Mexico and
Wyoming have only one or two inhabitants to the square mile. We are apt
to think of the settlement of thinly
populated territories only in terms of
agricultural development. Undoubtedly
the ploughshare and the pruning hook are
the first to follow on the heels of the
rifle and axe, but where, as in the United
States to-day, there is a steady seepage
of population from the country to the
town, it is only when the oil derrick, the
pick and the power line come upon the
scene that the business of human multipli-
cation really begins. There are vast
areas in the United States that still seem
destined to produce nothing in particular

but the natural resources of the country have by no means been fully investigated and human resource in making two blades of commercial prosperity grow where one grew before is unlimited. Within a few years Oklahoma was successively an Indian reservation, a farming state and a rapidly developing exporter of oil, coal and natural gas to the cities of the Cotton Belt.

Getting the right kind of settlers, or indeed any settlers at all, for large areas of virgin country, however productive it may promise to be, is a heartbreaking business. The would-be immigrant is generally the human surplusage and often the human detritus of some overcrowded industrial district. The city life is in his bones and if harsh necessity or some fleeting mood of adventure does send him into the wilderness, he either goes under or goes back to the city. Europe supplies about ninety-five per cent. of the world's migrants and Europe has long since ceased to teach men and women to bear loneliness or be self-reliant. And those who have learned the lesson are the least anxious to make use of their knowledge.

It is otherwise with migration to lands rich in industrial opportunity, that is to say to lands already reasonably populous and well supplied with cities, and

the little towns of to-day that are destined
to be the great cities of to-morrow.
These can get all the immigrants they
want, not only from Europe but from
the neighbouring agricultural areas that
supply their needs.   In the United
States, as elsewhere, there is a steady
movement of population from the country
to the towns which are also the objectives
of the vast proportion of the immigrants
from overseas.   In 1900 the population of
the United States was 33 per cent. urban, in
1920, 51 per cent. In 1900 the urban population of the States of Massachusetts, Maine,
Vermont, and Iowa was respectively
76, 24, 11, and 17 per cent.   In 1920 it was
95, 39, 31, and 36 per cent. The rush to
the cities is of course reflected in the
gain of industrialism at the expense of
local agriculture.   In 1900 improved land
in the New England states had decreased
to approximately 68 per cent. of what
it was in 1870.   By 1920 it has further
decreased to 51 per cent.

No elaborate explanation of this pheno-
menon is needed.   As matters are con-
stituted to-day alike in Europe and the
United States civilization, both material
and spiritual, stands on a higher plane
in the cities than in the country.   We may
think it need not be so.   We may feel
it ought not to be so.   We may believe
that we are rapidly reaching a point

where something will have to be done about it. At present, however, that is the fact, and it is a fact of prime importance where the future of the United States people is concerned.

There used to be a class of thinker— we may suspect him to have originated in Manchester—who used to talk about the population of England, surplus or otherwise as a " national asset " and of their industry (if they happened to be industrious) as " potential wealth." According to their doctrine you could not have too many people. *"Bella gerant alii, tu felix Lancastria proliferas"* might have been their motto. There were people in the United States who held similar views. These, in the throes of Fourth of July optimism or the annual banquet of the local Chamber of Commerce, looked forward to the day when the United States would have a population of seven hundred million. This vision involves among other unpleasant considerations the consumption by the inhabitants of North America of all the foodstuffs that are now exported to Europe. Fortunately it need not detain us for it has given way, in the American if not in the Manchester mind, to a more scientific theory.

This may be stated somewhat as follows. The consuming power of the individual is strictly limited. He can only eat so much food and sleep on one bed. He can only play on one piano at a time and listen-in on one radio set. The quantity of clothing, of building materials, of tools and implements and machinery and books that he can make use of is restricted. The dividing line between necessities and luxuries is reasonably constant, for the luxury of to-day that becomes the necessity of to-morrow, is counterbalanced by the necessity of yesterday that has passed entirely out of use. The point at which all the reasonable needs of all its citizens are fairly met has been reached in the United States. They are not content because all men naturally desire a share of the luxuries and amenities of life. It quickly appears, however, that these luxuries are not the gift of the Great God Production, that some of them, rare postage stamps and trout streams and old masters for example, are not susceptible of production at all, while others such as foreign travel, rare wines, beautifully printed books, race horses and so forth, though the subject of commercial production in a limited sense, involve an amount of labour that is negligible when compared with their cost.

When a self-contained community has reached the point where consumption can only just keep pace with production; and is exercising its maximum power of employment, a further influx of population is more likely to be a burden than an advantage. If they do not work they are a liability. If they work the fruits of their toil, being surplus to domestic requirements, must be sold abroad. But the power of exporting such surplus products is limited to a small margin above the equivalent of what the community will take in exchange. If the community is really self-contained it can take nothing in exchange that is any more valuable to it than its own surplus products. In actual fact no country is self-contained, so when the maximum of domestic consumption is reached a further margin of production must be allowed in order that there may be something to exchange for necessary imports.

The United States to-day has got enough people to produce sufficient for all its domestic requirements of the things it can produce, and to export in exchange for an adequate supply of the things it cannot produce. If another fifty million were added to its population to-morrow they too might be employed in producing enough for their own needs, but their coming could not in the nature of things be of the slightest material benefit to the hundred millions already *in situ*.

On the other hand, there are a score of ways in which they might be a great nuisance if nothing worse. They might lower the physique or the morale of the community. Many of them might turn out to be unemployable, and in any case the business of absorbing them into the productive life of the nation would be expensive. Their coming might have undesirable political consequences. The United States, having considered all these matters, have come to the conclusion that a further increase of the population by immigrants from elsewhere is not desirable. Since the war they have cut down the invading army of opportunity seekers to a maximum of less than one half the pre-war figure, and those best able to judge believe that within the next decade the door will be banged, bolted and barred in the face of Europe's surplus millions.

The moral of all this is that the population of the United States, which is twenty-seven times what it was a hundred and thirty years ago, is likely to increase during the next few decades at a much lower rate, so much so that it is most improbable that by 2000 A.D. it will have passed to 200,000,000 mark, an increase which should necessitate no fundamental readjustments of world trade or world politics. Cultivated Europeans,

accustomed to a world in which comparative handfuls of people have stamped their
exploits and the contributions to civilization deep into the rock face of history,
must envisage the threatened existence
of a solid mass of two hundred million
Americans with unqualified apprehension.
What a dent *they* in turn could make in
the surface of things once they set about
it, and how incapable they seem, at
present, of presenting a cutting edge to
the granite face that records nothing
futile or infirm ? At present the menace
is apparent only to the British, who
realise that with so many ideals and
institutions in common (a community
that their apprehension perhaps causes
them to exaggerate), a common literature
and a largely common language the
civilization two hundred million strong
is bound, no matter how formless or
erratic it may be, to absorb and destroy
the civilization of the forty million.
Some day, however, Europe will realise
that the American of the future is not
going to be merely a sort of hollow
ground, self-stropping, all-steel, Britisher,
but a super-Occidental capable, by virtue
of his infinite racial variety of impressing
his culture, for better or for worse, on
every European race that has contributed
to his polychromatic ancestry.

Of the present population of the United

States about thirteen per cent. are negroes, the bulk of whom are still concentrated in the Southern States. Once the negro was supposed to provide the great and insoluble problem that the American people would one day be called upon to face. Books were written about it, and at one time it provided a certain type of political orator with some useful ammunition. Even to-day it supplies a frequent excuse for the incitement and exercise of the sort of mob tyranny that is associated with the Ku Klux Klan. Quite unexpectedly and fortuitously an apparent solution of the problem has recently presented itself.

The curtailment of immigration and the new industrial boom coming soon after the war produced a shortage of unskilled labour in the manufacturing states, and the negroes began to move out of the Southern states in search of higher wages and more congenial work. At the same time a wave of industrial development and expansion commenced in the Southern states and skilled white labour began to flow in. The significance of this latter fact is apparent when we remember that in the fifty years preceding the war several million whites migrated from the South to the North and West.

The figures are rather astonishing. It is estimated that in one year alone,

c

1921-1922—half a million negroes got employment in the Northern mills. Between 1910 and 1920 every Southern state, instead of the 10-15 per cent. increase of previous decades showed a drop in the negro population of approximately four per cent. By 1924 South Carolina for the first time since the Civil War had a majority white population, and when Mississippi follows suit, as it will in the next two years, there will be no state in the Union with a population more than fifty per cent coloured.

The influx of whites to the new Southern industrial areas is less marked and to date has been rather an industrialization of the white agriculturists of the Appalachian valleys who have moved to Birmingham, Alabama, and the cotton-spinning centres of the Carolinas. Once 19/20ths of all the cotton goods manufactured in the United States were manufactured in the North. To-day the proportion is about 55% North and 45% South.

Scatter the negro throughout the whole of the United States and he ceases to be a political problem. He does, however, become more of a social problem because where there are only a comparatively few negroes it is proportionately more difficult to keep them in a social world of their own, to segregate them in coloured schools and universities and trade unions, and confine them by law or custom to their own ball parks, cinemas, residential districts and so forth. This is peculiarly true of the Northern industrial towns thickly populated with comparative new-comers from Middle and Southern Europe, who have not the same innate dislike to mixing with the coloured races that is felt by the older United States stock.

So far the thing has proceeded at haphazard and the people of the United States have not seriously asked themselves whether they definitely prefer the old policy of keeping the negro as far as possible confined to the Southern states, or the new policy of scattering him throughout the industrial areas of the whole United States as substitute for the unskilled labour hitherto imported from Europe. It is still possible that the American people may conclude that the latter policy is nationally injurious and adopt the only remedy of reopening the doors to the surplus European.

The question will take a lot of deciding and the many pros and cons cannot be elaborated here. The facts that cannot be ignored are that the negro increases much faster than the white American, that there are vast and immensely fertile areas in the Cotton Belt where the white man is debarred from settling and multiply-ing by climatic conditions and that the negroes are making extraordinary progress in the acquisition of both property and education.

The blood that flows in the veins of the white American people is a mixture in varying proportions of the blood of all the races of Europe most of whom are themselves unanalysable *melanges* of diversified tribes, races, conquering aristocracies and what not. It is claimed to be Anglo-Saxon or British in origin to the extent of fifty-two per cent., but this figure is greatly exaggerated. It is certain however that if we leave out of account not only the unassimilated races, negro, Chinese and Japanese, but also the Middle East and South European hordes that have swarmed into the United States into the last few decades and have not yet had time to be absorbed, we find the blood of the American people to be preponderatingly Anglo-Saxon, Irish and German.

But what will be the position in, let us say, seventy-five years from now ? In the first place all the millions of Russians, Greeks, Poles, Portuguese, Italians, Slovaks and miscellanous Mittel-Europeans who have reached the Land of Opportunity in the last thirty years or so will have become unidentifiably absorbed in the mass of the population. In the first few decades after their arrival in a new country races always tend to "keep themselves to themselves," as the charladies say, but this does not last long and is generally the result of economic conditions. In Massachusetts at the present time we find one city with Irish as its prevailing foreign element, another close to it with Portuguese, another with Italian, a fourth with French Canadian and so forth.

The initial herding together of the alien, however, causes his conquest of the country to proceed slowly, for he tends to make one town or one province thoroughly his own before proceeding to the next. That he will be able to proceed to the next, even if the ban on immigration should be made complete (and in one case—that of the Irish— the quota is still sufficiently large to allow of an influx of 20,000 per annum), is due to the fact that he multiplies about twice as fast as the native born American. In 1910 the foreign born population of Connecticut was 30 per cent. and gave birth to 63 per cent. of the children. One explanation of this is due to the fact that the incoming foreigners are about ninety per cent. Roman Catholic and the Roman Catholic church forbids birth control with the full weight of its doctrinal and moral authority. So the Irish, the French Canadians, the

Italians and Portuguese and Poles and Slovenes, multiply exceedingly while the native white stock, when it does not go West, dies out. One pessimistic American writer declares that the native stock is " melting away about as fast as the Indian melted away before the white man's advance."

The following passage from Professor J. Russell Smith's " North America " under the cross heading " Exit the Puritan " gives an idea of the present state of the Melting Pot in New England :

" A Colleague in Harvard tells me that on a Sunday afternoon in spring one may hear on Boston Common ' every language but English.' There are places in New England towns where the stores have signs ' English spoken here.' An investigator spent an hour in the city hall of Woonsocket, R.I. during which time he heard no English except that which was addressed to him. The shop committee in a Peabody tannery in 1918 had the following rich variety : two Greeks, two Irish-Americans, one Pole, one Portuguese, one Italian, one Turk, two of unidentified foreign nationality. In the list of sons of New Britain, Conn. who died overseas the names beginning with S were as follows : Sarisky,

Schade, Schleicher, Senf, Siomakevicz, Skorupa, Smith, Sokovich, Strohecher, Stunia, Sullivan, Sullivan."

The births and deaths recorded in one month of 1915 in a New England manufacturing town show the following names : Births ;   Perline, Musante, Kottman, Balster, Dictk, Groszek, Smey, Kempt, Govin,   Moriscato,   Styfcka,   Borcz, Nasiadka.   Deaths :   Simpson, Piper, Losee, Goodall, Wyant, Blum (aged one month).

These fast breeding swarms of Continental-born newcomers are exclusively urban. Though many of them come of agricultural stock it is the American cities that attract them and there they settle as industrial workers,   peddlars,   small   shopkeepers, policemen, domestic servants, gardeners, street cleaners, as taste and temperament and race incline them.   Often a single race   contrives   to   secure   a   practical monopoly in one kind of job. All the New York policemen are Irish, all the street cleaners   Italian.   Greeks specialise in quick lunch counters.   The negro monopolises the businesses of janitor and pullman car attendant.   The Italians follow their time-honoured   occupations   of   selling bananas, grinding organs and tending the gardens of the well-to-do.   The native born has a prescriptive right to enter any of these occupations but as yet he does not find it necessary. He is still the Man at the Top, the store owner and bank manager the political boss the captain and director of the vast industrial machine. Education and the dissemination of know-lege—not by any means identical fields of endeavour in the United States—are also his virtual monopoly, his only rival herein being the negro. For the rest he still follows Horace Greely's advice and moves West before the invading hordes, taking his brains and enterprise—and his procreative diffidence—along with him. The last American who can trace his descent back through five generations of wholly Anglo-Saxon ancestors will expire somewhere about 2025 A.D. in the island of Guam.

Of these proliferous newcomers, of the Irish, the Jew, the Italian, the Croat, the Pole, the Greek and the Slav, is to be built the great American civilization that is to come. They are raw material in every sense of the word, a *tabula rasa* on which anything may be written. The United States has already a history but it is not their history. It has a literature but it is not their literature. It has old customs and traditions, old ties of senti-ment, songs and tales and jests racy of the soil and the people who tilled it, of the pioneers who went forth into the wilder-ness and conquered it. They are not an inheritance of the people that are making America to-day. Nor does Europe mean anything more to them. These newcomers to the Land of Liberty were the hewers of wood and the drawers of water, the *kannonfutter* alike of peace and war, in the lands whence they came. They became Americans the day they reached Ellis Island. The great war shook them all mightily, reviving old, dim race antagonisms and international jealousies, setting the German to hate the French, the Italian to conspue the Slav, the Pole to thirst for the blood of the Prussian and the Irish to conspire against the British. The United States went into the war belatedly but as a people that had wrestled mightily with itself and become united in the process. So, at least, it is said, though others claim that it was the native born, money-controlling, educated Anglo-Saxons that compelled the die to be cast. In any case the people of the United States will never again look towards Europe with anything resembling emotion. They may allow their rulers to throw their weight about a bit in world politics. They may even take part in some punitive expedition organised by the League of Nations if that curious organization should survive. But they will never again allow themselves to take sides, one side or all sides, in a European squabble. For

[41]

America the great war really was a war to end war.

Out of this raw material, out of these negative millions, the new American civilization will one day be built up. We can hardly guess what it will be but we can at least see the direction in which the things of the American spirit seem to be moving.

Chapter II

THE FUTURE OF
AMERICAN GOVERNMENT

As the preoccupations and interests of a people become more numerous and more varied their interest in politics—other then the frenetic but intermittent excitement of the hustings—wanes. In an Ireland or a Mexico, where recreations are scarce and the standard of living low, where physical isolation is the order of the day and ignorance disputes the sway of that most efficient broadcaster of intellectual diversion, the printing press, everybody is a politician.

In the primitive communal life of the post-Revolutionary American people politics, local and national, were a matter of general concern, not the hectic and usually futile politics of peoples who are primitive because they are uncivilized but the well deliberated and constructive politics of a community with a thousand years of sound constitutional experience behind it.

It is a far cry from the Select Men of De Toqueville's era to the Tammany ward boss of our own, but the gulf is not as great as might be imagined. If the fellow citizens of Washington, Madison and Jefferson had had gramophones, wireless, motor cars, roof gardens, golf courses, beach clubs, and all the other Persian apparatus of our high speed age, not to mention the libraries, museums, magazines, cheap tours and still cheaper education that do so much or so little to broaden our intellectual life, they too would have left the comparatively tedious business of politics to the professional politicians, the men who play the game of politics for what there is in it. It may be urged that there were no professional politicians in those Arcadian days. We may suspect however that it only required a little encouragement to bring them forward. Professional politics is the only trade in which no apprenticeship need be served and there is always plenty of room at the bottom. Moreover professionalism in politics is not as well defined as it is in Lawn tennis. The gilding on the helm of state is primarily intended for purposes of ornament but it easily comes off on the hands.

Thoughtful students of constitutional law and history both in England and America concede that the British governing machine is more efficient than the American, that it is quicker, less expensive, gets a larger percentage of results with less noise and vibration. Various explanations are offered, the commonest being that while the British people are still essentially the people for whom and by whom the British governing system was devised, General Washington and company could not by any means have imagined, when they framed the American Constitution, the sort of posterity they were actually making it for. It is also pointed out that the British grew their constitution as an animal grows its skin while the American people were per force compelled to acquire one *uno ictu* like a ready-to-wear suit of clothes. Neither explanation is adequate. In the first place constititions —even the so called rigid ones—can be changed and expanded to meet the new needs or the changing outlook of a people and in the second place the United States Constitution was only ready-made in a limited sense since it was, or at least was intended to be, merely a modification of the British system of government— with which the framers were, in general, quite satisfied—designed to meet certain exigencies forced upon the American colonies by that egregious German lunatic, King George III.

The real explanation of why the American system of government as we see it to-day is far behind the British system in

efficiency and an astonishing contrast to
American efficiency in general is that
the Americans reached the present peak
of material civilization too quickly with
the result that instead of continuing to
shape and mould their laws and constitutions nearer to their hearts' desires they
abandoned themselves to more attractive
pursuits leaving it to the professional
politicians to do the moulding, not merely
according to their hearts' desires but
according to their pockets' requirements.
The British Constitution was in the making
for a thousand years before the British
people had added to the three primitive
pursuits of man—food, fighting and
females—any substantial addition besides
politics and the consolations of their
religion which by the end of the period
had become largely political in character.
To these the English country gentleman
of the early sixteenth century could add
an occasional yarn with a travelled
stranger, a little chamber music a little
crude drama and a restricted dip, if
he had an enquiring mind, into botanical
medicine. For the rest he firmly believed
that the hairs from horses' tails turned
into eels and devoted himself to governing
and being governed with a maximum
of justice and a minimum of inconvenience.
To these inborn desires—to have justice
and avoid discomfort—must be attributed

all that the Englishman is, all that he possesses and all that he has ever done. The modern American, who mistakes legalism for justice and dislikes it and who seldom has a comfortable chair in his house (he has only just begun to abandon that gymnasium on the hearth, the rocking chair), is more remote from him in his fundamental outlook on life than the Chinaman.

One has only to glance at the American constitutional system and in particular at the political systems that prevail in the various states to realise that America is the professional politician's paradise. The presence in the States of vast numbers of Irish—the world's most industrious but most inartistic exponents of graft and corruption—is thought to account for this. Had they been absent we may suppose that some more finished and picturesque system would have replaced their crude dominion, something not less profitable to the politicians but less expensive because efficiency and artistry are always less expensive 'than coarseness and crudity. At the close of the great war Britain was the scene of one huge concatenated orgy of public plunder, nepotism, backscratching, title buying, indemnity-mongering and plain graft. But it was all done most pleasantly. There was no fuss in the newspapers, no scandal.

The dirty work was not allowed to obtrude and the British public wisely decided that once the plunder was all shared out the world would turn honest again and that it would only aggravate matters to make a row about it.

The professional politician is more of a nuisance in the United States than elsewhere because he has made over the American political system to suit himself and without regard to the real needs of the people. Those who take pleasure in reminding themselves on sundry occasions that "that sort of thing could not happen in England" must recollect that it is our system which restrains our professional politicians and not our professional politicians that restrain themselves.

But will the Americans allow their present system to continue and develop? They are an efficient people. Will they not revolt and say to the professional politicians "We accept you but we insist that you too shall be efficient, that you shall have your hire and be worthy of it." As a matter of fact that is just what the American people are everlastingly doing. There is not a big city in the United States that has not had a dozen " reform " tickets, " clean up " campaigns, " good government " agitations, whose leading citizens, stung beyond endurance, have not momentarily torn themselves away

from the golf club and the counting house
to prance to the polls with the slogan
" Kick the Irish (or Tammany Hall or the
Southern Pacific Railroad or the Oil
Magnates or some other gang or interest)
out of politics ! "

No permanent results are achieved
because the reformers merely attack the
politicians and not the system. The
politicians knowing that as long as
they control the system nothing very
serious can happen to them, disappear
into the tall grass until the hunters, weary
of their futile sport, desist, and then emerge
and make up for lost time by ravaging the
political melon patch with twice their
previous zeal. They do not want to be
worthy of their hire or to have a limit
put upon their possible receipts. And
because the people of the United States
are every day finding new and more
attractive pursuits, alike for pleasure and
profit, and are becoming proportionately
less inclined to concern themselves with
politics there is every indication that for
a while yet the professional politicians
will have things their own way.

The ideal of the framers of the Constitution was that the people should elect the
most suitable men to conduct the nation's
political business and the elected should
thereupon proceed to perform their duties
conscientiously and without reference to

[49]   D

the opinions or individual interests of their
electors. From that ideal the American
people have steadily departed. First
they made the representative a mere
delegate. The Electoral College, for
example, which was intended originally
to choose a President, became a cumber-
some apparatus for nominating formally
a President already chosen by the vote
of the people. The selection of United
States Senators was originally intended
to rest with the State legislatures but they
too have in most cases become the mere
mouthpieces through which the choice of
the people is confirmed. Once elected,
however, no ministerial responsibility
bound the Executive and no party
responsibility bound Congressmen or State
legislators to the promotion of any
particular measure or programme. Legis-
lation became a matter of swapping
favours between individual legislators,
each of whom had no real interest save
that of appeasing his constituents by
securing some advantage to them. To get
something of advantage to themselves
is the hope and aim of all constituencies
but whereas in a small country like
Britain identity of interest quickly welds
the wishes of the constituents into the
wishes of the party, whereupon the
political machinery promptly converts it
into a plank in the party platform, in the

United States there are so many constituents and so vast a diversity of interests that there is never a sufficient identity of ideas among all the constituencies to form a party at all.

The result in the United States was a government in which the representatives fought for their constituencies alone and the so called parties were merely convenient but meaningless labels by which the voters might identify themselves in order to have their noses counted and not as an indication of anything they might be supposed to want or to think. A Republican is theoretically one who wants more Federal power, a Democrat, one who desires the enlargement of the State's functions. The issue has been dead sixty years. At one time it was thought that the Republican stood for a high tariff, the Democrat for a low tariff. In 1912 more than half the Republican Party broke away and became moderate tariff Progressives while of the Democrats it became obvious when they went into power that each was for protecting the interests of his own constituency with a high tariff while demanding free trade for everybody else. To-day the party names mean nothing and the struggle is not one of competing ideals or grabbing but between two opposing gangs of politicians to come to anchor within grabbing distance of the " pie counter."

The next step which the American people took with the idea of being able to make the desires of the majority law within a measurably shorter space of time was the adoption of the Initiative and the Referendum. These carry government of the people by the people and (in intention at least) for the people to their logical extremity and throw into sharpest relief the distinction between the supposed American ideal of Democracy and the British conception of it as a system under which " the will of the people *ultimately* prevails."

They have not been a success in America. They do indeed provide a method by which the majority's will can at any moment be made to prevail and that not only in general terms but by line, section and clause, but they also demand of the citizen the concentration and attention that he prefers to lavish elsewhere. Psychologically the modern American is in a very peculiar position as regards government and its major manifestation, the enforcement of the law. He wants to be governed vicariously *and* efficiently but can do neither with his present machinery. He has no respect for the law, with the making and enforcement of which he does not consider himself to be identified, but flatly refuses to step in and take such political

action as will make him feel that in obeying
the law he is merely following his own
wishes. The result is a series of spasmodic
and futile inhibitions (for which the
American has a marked taste—a legacy
from the old Puritan stock) such as
Prohibition and Fundamentalism, which
will certainly become the law of the United
States if the great industrialists once
conclude that it will add some fraction
of one per cent to the efficiency of their
workers and put up the money to make
it law.

This mania for passing laws making
themselves do things by numbers is the
most striking feature of modern American
life. It is a manifestation of the spirit
that makes them yell for their college
teams to the beat of the baton and inspires
the meaningless "exercises" of their
innumerable secret societies. It will
become more and more a feature of the
American political system and for that
reason the system is bound to be greatly
changed in the next fifty years.

The truth is that the modern American
has no use for liberty and liberty plays
no part in what he conceives to be democracy. He conspues the imaginary tyranny
of kings and emperors but earnestly
desires to replace them with the very
real tyranny of the fifty-one per cent.
He wants the will or whim of the fifty-one

per cent. to become law at once and
without qualification. Just at present
he is more willing to pass the laws ordering
himself to do this and not to do that than
he is to go through the motions themselves
but he will acquire the habit of obedience,
or rather of not wanting to do what he
wants himself not to want to do, soon
enough. But he does not want to be
bothered with law making or law enforc-
ing. He wants his vote to sway all things,
like Jove, with its nod but he wants his
political machine to be an automatic
machine into which he drops his vote and
out comes another slab of uplift or a
neat packet of industrial efficiency or
shouts of delight from a Europe made
brighter and better at the ridiculously
low rate of two and three quarter cents
on the dollar.

The present system does not work
in this way. Often the penny takes a
long time to drop. It took eighteen
months for the people of the United
States formally to register their disapproval of the Versailles Treaty during
which period they were prepared to take
the deepest umbrage at any suggestion
that President Wilson was not and should
not be accepted by Europe as the Big
Noise. At other times the penny drops
but the package delivered is found to

contain lemon drops and be labelled " A Present from Big Business."

So the change will come, not easily because the professional politicians are strongly entrenched and will fight desperately, but inevitably. The Judiciary will be taken out of politics, cities will be governed by paid bodies of expert Commissioners, Federal, State, County and Municipal employees will come one by one under the purview of Civil Service Commissions until finally a Board of professors from Harvard and elsewhere will select as President of the United States the man who passes the necessary examination with the highest marks. Probably they will add to their first award a footnote to the effect that judged by the most exhaustive psychological tests the candidates' composite capacity for reacting to mass impulse is considerably below that of the average peddler of patent medicine. And the legislator will of course be abolished. The voter will receive by punctual post a copy of each new measure that the Federal or State legislative experts think should become law. He will write in the place appointed " Yes " or " No " (having carefully read the directions cautioning him against writing both or signing his name with a rubber stamp) and return it whence it came. Two weeks later he will learn that

[55]

the measure has duly become law. A month later he will flagrantly violate its provisions. An efficient policeman with a university degree will refuse ten dollars to condone the offence, an honest District Attorney will decline, at the instance of a friend of the accused with a political pull, to quash the proceedings, a high minded judge with whom the accused plays bridge daily at the club will sum up heavily against him and a jury of stout fellows who have all committed precisely the same offence several times within the last week, will bring in a verdict of guilty. He will be removed, amid applause, to a month's hard labour in the State Institution for the Treatment of Persons deficient in Civism.

Chapter III

THE FUTURE OF
AMERICAN CHARACTER

What are the things that build up human character and give individuality to the race? First and foremost climate and environment. The degraded marsh Arabs of Mesopotamia are one in race and blood with the men who built the Alhambra and taught the world astronomy and medicine. The snake worshipping Hopi Indians are of the blood of the Incas. Like the Colonel's lady and Judy O'Grady, all the races of Europe are " sisters under their skins." History should but does not in fact provide an explanation of the way in which environment and accident together have made them into innumerable races, each with its own language, its own racial individuality and its own physical characteristics. An investigation of these circumstances can only be superficial but it suggests that we should hesitate to assume that the people of the United States are a solid body all moving in one given direction. To-day the Californian is simply a Middle Westerner who has moved to California. The Middle Westerner is the Easterner who has gone West. It will not always be that way though many decades must elapse before the Westerly drift of the human flotsam ceases to be important. Someday however the people of the South Western United States—the men on whom the snow does *not* fall—must begin to grow into a race as different from the hard living, cold enduring North Easterner as the Neapolitan is from the Swede and much further removed from him than the old Southern slave owner was from the hard-faced Yankees of Salem and New Bedford.

It will take a long time because civilization has done much to discount environment. The railway, the steamboat, and the motor car have done away with geographical isolation. Clothes and food and customs have ceased to be " local colour " except for the purpose of interesting tourists. The sweater knitted by the Fair Island cottager adorns the torso of the golfer in Honolulu and *chile con carne* is served in Soho. Mosul bulks large in the day's paper to millions the world over who never think of it as the place where muslin came from. Modern science and machinery are standardized the world over and education tends to become so.

Architecture is still local but the two-step has gone through the Northern races like measles through a slum. Geographical environment remains though even here man has broken down some of the barriers. He has learned to tackle the mosquito which has probably had more to do with the building up and destruction of Empires and civilizations than war and religion rolled into one. Some day he will learn to build refrigerated cities in the tropics as he now builds steam heated cities in the lands of frost and snow and then the reign of modern civilization will no longer be confined to the temperate zones.

In spite of all that has been done to discount it, environment will remain a controlling factor, however, in the moulding of racial character and we must look to it to establish in time distinct race groups among the people of the United States. That is looking very far ahead, however, and strange things may happen in the meantime. Civilization has not in the past been a thing of persistent growth. We are told to attribute its disappearance on this occasion or that to obvious phenomena, barbarian invasions, the shifting of trade-routes, wars and pestilences, and what not. The fact that people at long periods get fed up with civilization, which they feel is getting to be, as it were, one too many for them, and lose interest in it and begin first to mark time and then to move backwards towards a less complicated and exacting life, is ignored. The fact remains and we may not refuse to entertain the possibility of a wholesale and drastic revolt by the human race against the civilization of to-day which threatens to enthrone the power plant and the machine and make of man an ant toiling in a hill, a robot functioning according to plans over which he has long lost all control. Nature before now has wiped the slate clean and begun again and so has man himself. It is impossible to regard the United States without coming to the conclusion that it is there the great revolt will come because there the breaking strain will be reached, the tyranny of a power-driven civilization become intolerable.

America is to-day the land of many and efficient machines, the one place where machines are suffered gladly and even welcomed enthusiastically by all sections of the community. In the old world some bitterness and hostility is still expressed. The machine, we point out, was introduced and encouraged in the belief that as it could do the work of anything from three to a hundred men a life of opulent ease lay before us all. To-day with the machine working its hardest we find ourselves also working harder than ever before in our lives, hampered with an incredible number of material possessions, gadgets, utilities and other highly specialized objects that bring no happiness into our lives and still actuated by a far greater number of unsatisfied desires than ever before.

These considerations do not move the European to anything but painful reflections but they do not actuate the American at all. He glories in life's physical complexity, hugs his chain, fondles the machine that is gnawing his vitals. In a factory in Chicago which employed child labour there used to be posted notices " Do not waste the machine's time." The modern minotaur must be fed at all costs ! At present America is nothing like so factory-ridden as England but there the farmer has also come under the sway of the machine. So it comes about that the American mind is also becoming a machine, one in which the undisciplined processes of reflection and ratiocination and imagination are falling into disuse and thought is becoming an apparatus for registering the readymade idea or translating it into action.

The most striking thing about the young Americans of to-day is that they know nothing and have no ideas of their own. No matter what they learn in college they remember nothing of it for the simple reason that the things learned at school and

college that come under the general head of
education are of no use except as pegs
on which to hang ideas, pawns to push
about on the chessboard of thought.

The American does not want to think
and is rapidly forgetting how to think.
He is living more and more in two dimen-
sions, length and breadth with no depth.
He wants all the potentialities of life to
be analysed for him and to be handed a
booklet in which every opinion he may be
called upon to hold and every course of
action he may be required to pursue can
be immediately found by referring to
page three or chapter six. Such books
the American does in fact consult though
they are of limited scope. The vade
mecum in which the whole gamut of
life and thought is reduced to rules and
definitions, like a manual of infantry
training, has yet to appear. The young
vendor of insurance is instructed through
a book or by means of lectures exactly
how to behave in the presence of his
victims, which hand to hold his hat in,
what to say as he opens the door, when
not to spit on the carpet and so on. He
is taught a series of openings—a line of
talk—which he can follow with the
blind precision of a chess player.

It is quite unimportant whether intensive business has induced in the American
a ready-to-wear mind or whether he

has deliberately jettisoned all mental processes that interfere with the stark business of turning effort into money. The fact remains that every year young America tends more and more to do its living and its thinking by numbers. Young men determined to get on must acquire a car by hook or by crook because it is decreed that no young man can hope to get on without one. When the time comes to go about in society they apply themselves more studiously than ever at college to the business of acquiring a "line." This can be bought in a book and though in this case the word "line" is said to be an abbreviation of "life line" the rules exactly resemble those with which the young vendor of insurance or patent medicine starts forth, only that society dames are substituted for buyers and departmental managers and apposite remarks about the weather, the latest from Tin Pan alley, the activities of the Daughters of the Revolution or a new bunch of peppy slang are substituted to taste for mesmeric eulogies of the properties of shaving soap, canned goods and steel frame windows.

This tendency to live superficially, to shun all mental processes not tending to immediate action and despise knowledge that cannot be put to immediate practical use has been many years developing but has gained great momentum in the last twenty years. It manifested itself early in a desire to substitute a purely technical or vocational education for the merely educative scholastic course of the older universities. The student was no longer content to have a technical training administered on purely technical branches of knowledge, chemistry and engineering and agriculture, or to emerge from his alma mater a full-blown lawyer or doctor or pedagogue. He wished—and was soon enabled—to take his degree in journalism, in finance and finally in advertising and salesmanship. There the thing has stopped because to the American these two occupations—publicity and salesmanship—represent the peak of desirable human efficiency. Only one step further can be taken—if it has not already been taken as an integral part of one of the existing curricula. A degree in Social Adequacy has still to be bestowed. There is no reason why it should not be for already it has become almost as exact a science as chemistry and already the social side of American university life is as stereo-typed as was that of an early Victorian debutante. A modern young American who on leaving the University could not dance, drive a car, play one or more instruments in a jazz band and, when need arose, lay his hands on the makings of

[64]

a cocktail would be something of a *lusus naturae*.

The result of all this is that though the United States have countless universities, one of which has over twenty thousand students, they have no educated class outside of their college professors who rank in the social scale a little higher than the average preacher and a little lower than the average bootlegger.

As good a test of a community's culture as any is furnished by its publishers' catalogues. More books on natural history, botany and country life generally are published every year in England than have been published in the United States since the Mayflower landed there. The same is true of almost every other branch of literature outside of fiction. The explanation is simple. Reading is either a hobby, in nine cases out of ten, or the essential adjunct of a hobby. And whereas it is quite unusual to find an educated Englishman who has not a hobby of some sort it is the exception to find an American who has. For his business is his hobby while the European mind still regards the day's work as something of a curse and Adam a fool for having brought it on us all.

This does not mean that young America cannot amuse itself. On the contrary it has, when not working, a riotously good

time but that good time is not allowed
to employ the brain. Dancing, motoring,
swimming, skating, theatre parties and
beach parties—Americans do everything
in parties—movies and wireless and sing
songs and jazz bands, and picnics, and
so on—life can be one long glad round
of these and still seem quite full. In an
older country, a country with less sunshine,
and more care in it, these Sybaritic
preoccupations tend to grow garish and
tedious. Young America is so full of
life and "pep," so brimming with an
enthusiasm which its dyspeptic elders
do not share, that it seems quite natural
and sufficient for it to live on the surface
of things. Dancing as aimlessly as gnats
in winter sunshine it yet brings to bear
on the jolly business of being *ephemeridae*
the same hard and cheerful efficiency that
it uses in its money making. American
jazz bands and vaudeville shows that
come to Europe have about them a snap
and "jizz" that has won Europe in spite
of itself. America is immensely alive
and its horizon is unlimited. It is only
intellectual expansion that is limited by a
thousand considerations of time, place,
money, the distractions of business and
what not. The grasshopper life never
lacks variety and its only drawback is
that sooner or later one ceases to be able
to hop. That drawback is simply solved

in the United States. They wear out their nerves quicker than their legs. They have only two classes there, the quick and the dead.

Two other influences are doing much to mould the character of the young American of to-day. The first of these is Standardization. Standardization means monotony. It is the negation of individualism and the result if not the actual aim alike of Socialism and that intensive form of Capitalism that Americans refer to as " Big Business." It has an atrophying effect on Art, the expression of which is largely if not wholly the reaction of the mind to material objects. In the modern industrial life, moreover, where all sorts of inhibitions restrict pursuit of the three primitive and still important sources of pleasure, food, fighting and females, life is largely enhanced by the multiplicity and variety of small material things. A nation that has twenty kinds of socks to choose from is better off than one that has only two. The Englishman who can still compare the output of *his* hatter and *his* tailor with those of his neighbour is leading a fuller life, *ceteris paribus*, than the American who simply buys the standard hat from a hat shop and the standard suit of clothes from the gents' furnishing department.

If the hiatus created by the elimination

[67]

in the sacred interests of business, of all types of objects and articles save one were to be filled by spiritual or aesthetic interests or by the pursuit of knowledge there would be nothing to complain about. A nation could get along with only one kind of socks if it were compensated with an extra large variety of tulips or frescoes or poetry magazines. It does not happen that way for the reason that all art is at bottom commercial or has a commercial side. The commercial instinct that eliminated all but one type of socks will also produce a million cheap copies of a single masterpiece and sell them to countless householders who would otherwise adorn their walls with the works of the village artist.

It may be urged that as long as people have money to spend they will demand novelties to spend it on. That is true and at the present day countless Americans are spending in Europe money that they cannot spend at home because there is nothing there they want to buy. Countless others, however, are using their money to make more money—enlarging the commercial snowball—for the same reason. This use of money—to make more money—is becoming standardized too.

The other influence of supreme importance is the American's mania for inhibitions.

If it is to be regarded as a cause we may ascribe it to the influence of the Pilgrim Fathers. If it is a result it is of course the result of the national desire to increase business efficiency by doing everything else by numbers. The two prime instances of the mania are Prohibition and Fundamentalism. America is full of fanatics— if you must take a little time off from minding your own business the most congenial alternative is to mind your neighbour's—but it is also full of people who resent restraint and enjoy cocktails. The former could never have overcome the latter and produced the necessary political action if merely moral and social aspects of the drink question had been at stake. Prohibition won because the fanatics made it clear to Big Business that while it, Big Business, would always be able to get its cocktail, the artisan would not be able to pay the price with the result that his value as a productive machine would be worth some small per cent more to Big Business than it was under the saloon regime. The Fundamentalist question started with the Tennessee legislators making a brave stand for freedom of belief. They took the stand that as between having their children's beliefs moulded by a lot of egg-headed scientists in German universities and having them regulated by

the laws of Tennessee they much preferred
the latter. The vast majority of the
American people, however, are recon-
reconciled to Evolution and have no
quarrel with Science which scatters
machines and fertilizers with a fatherly
hand. Why then will Fundamentalism
win out in the United States? It will
win because and when Big Business
decides that the productive efficiency of
the man machine that accepts the Bible
as written is one tenth of one per cent.
higher than it is at present when he
pauses intermittently from wielding his
shovel to ask himself unanswerable
questions about the Macrocosm. To
the Fanatics will fall the task of per-
suading Big Business that " Fundamentalism pays "—O magic slogan—and
no one who knows the American uplifter,
male and female, doubts their ability to
do it.

And the American will accept the law
to believe in the Bible as she is written
and break it whenever it suits him. It
is not so much that he does not want to
think as that he does not want to have to
think if he does not want to. He wants a
line of thought or action he can follow
without having to think about it but with
perfect propriety; as one of the crowd.
If he wants to think or act for himself
all he has to do is to break the law—a

thing no American hesitates to do if it suits his purpose.

Because men always follow the line of least resistance the habit of acting and believing " by numbers " will become stronger and assertions of individual freedom of action will become fewer. This is what the champions of Prohibition bank on when they declare that after a while America will become reconciled to a drinkless existence. As long as the law remains on the statute book the American cannot take a drink without calling mental processes into play. He will in the end decide that it is simpler (and more profitable) to stay dry and reserve his mental processes for money making.

Chapter IV

THE INTELLECTUAL FUTURE
OF AMERICA

America has not, at present any
civilization of its own. In intellectual
matters it is a pale reflection of Europe.
Its great painters are essentially European
painters. It draws its serious literature
from Europe, its own contribution of
historians, biographers, essayists, drama-
tists, and poets being negligible in quality
if not in quantity. In the decorative arts
America follows or draws from Europe.
Her women are dressed from Paris, her
domestic architecture and landscape gar-
dening are based on British and Italian
models.

On the other hand the beginnings of
an individual American civilization are
being made. By the time the Melting
Pot has produced the perfect American,
as it will do once all the ingredients are
finally poured in, the American civilization will be in full swing. Already American material civilization has hardened in
certain directions into a definite mould and

here already the seed of intellectual civilization is germinating. The skyscraper, for example, is the one new thing in architecture for a hundred years or more. So far it has only arrived commercially. What the architect can do with this new art form has yet to be seen. California is also creating a domestic architecture of its own wherein old forms are modified to the needs of environment and temperament. It is the same with Jazz. Tin Pan Alley already embodies in its brisk and frenetic cacophonies the restless and superficial but eminently vital spirit of young America. So far there has been no serious attempt to develop this new musical form beyond the needs of the dance hall. That too will come. Jazz is the foundation upon which America will build a redoubtable school of music if indeed Europe does not " get there first."

Painting is the one art that is wholly dissociated with material inspiration. For that reason it is largely international in scope. If it takes on a national cast it is the result, not of temperament, but environment. If there had been no Fuji there would have been no Hokusai. There are more Spanish atmospherics than Spanish character. The development of the pictorial art in America has been secondary for no one big reason

but for a number of small reasons. Europe
still monopolizes the market for exactly
the same reason that Britain has mono-
polized the motor cycle market. If New
York and Chicago have not their famous
ateliers it is simply because Paris has too
firm a hold of the business. Incidentally
Europe is stuffed full of ancient, mediaeval,
modern and futurist art. You can hardly
turn a street corner without running into
it. All the old masters and funiture and
Chinese ware and tapestries and illumin-
ated manuscripts and what not that
have been imported into the United
States by wealthy Americans can be
multiplied ten times over and still they
will have to be searched for to be seen and
nine out of ten Americans will go through
life without having cast an eye on them.
Their own environment will of course
improve as the years go by but slowly.
Very few American cities of any size
to-day are less than seventy-five years
old but few of them have yet cleared
their principal streets of forests of uncouth
telegraph poles. Europe however, though
it benefits by, can take no credit for the
past. Utilitarian art is fast losing vitality
in Europe. It may well be that America
having no other to console itself with,
will advance as quickly, once the spirit
moves it, as we are falling behind. It

has the energy and the money. All it requires is the desire for beauty.

If the face of America becomes defined on lines differing from anything existing elsewhere, an American Art, as distinct from that of Europe as is Chinese and Japanese art, may be evolved. It is a wide subject of speculation for already the most modern schools of painting—if one may call it that—profess to be uninfluenced by the superficial appearance of things. They paint states of mind. If that is so they should already be making headway in the America where the composite state of mind is immensely different from what it is in any other part of the world.

In Literature, America lags for the same reason that has impeded Chinese literature. They speak one language and write another. The American speaks American—a crisp, virile, colourful language full of copious possibilities—and writes English which he does not really understand. A double misfortune results. American literature suffers. Its one bright spot is fiction. The Americans are producing in bulk the best short stories and the most finished novels in the world. The reason is plain. They have magnificent material to hand, they can make their characters speak as God (or Uncle Sam) intended them and the author himself is granted a far greater license than if he were writing history or poetry.

American poetry is vile. Nothing so readily reflects the temperament of a people as its poetry and the American passion for *vers libre* is simply a reflection of American superficiality. It is a triumph of the business instinct over the creative instinct. Cut out rhyme and rhythm and you can churn out many more foot pounds of poetry at half a dollar a line than if you stop to polish the rough hewn jewels of thought until they shine again. That is the only explanation of *vers libre*, which has run through American literary circles like an epidemic. It enables you to get the money without earning it. Doubtless the American poet cultivates on the side powers of aggressive salesmanship that the English bard is without. There have been slight attempts to write American poetry but only one, that of Vachell Lindsey, has created any stir, His verse is intended for the platform. not for the fireside chair. He is a *jongleur*. The idea is good. At present American women still read poetry but in twenty years from now ten times as much poetry will be recited, over the wireless or otherwise, than will ever be read. By reading it the American can turn the

English into American as he goes and so impart the prescribed " kick " that such poems as " The Golden Whales of California " just miss as mere literature. Even so there is something wanting and what is wanting is the American's paralyzing lack of vocabulary and obvious desire to get through life with as few words as possible and in many cases to substitute for words a series of meaningful grunts. The grunting is the outcome of using the telephone for which the young American has invented a sort. of morse code, one grunt,two grunts, long and short, short and long, low and high, and so on and so forth according to whether they mean " Yes," " No," " I get you," " Quit yer kiddin' " and so on.

I have said that the American language as spoken is crisp and virile, full of colour and capable of great development. So it is, but instead of trying to develop it the American seems bent on reducing it to a bare minimum. All that O. Henry and George Ade have done, all the efforts of George Henry Lewis and Ring Lardner and Octavius Roy Cohen and a score of other argot-makers, have failed to get the American interested in his speech as such. The idea of brightening life by using or, preferably, misusing two words where he used one before simply does not appeal to him. If you

[77]

want to hear a bright vocabulary in America to-day you must go to the negroes or to the fast disappearing cow men and hill billies and lumber jacks, roughnecks of the old school who, like Cockney soldiers, never hear a new word without wanting to embellish their own speech with it.

America has many clever wielders of the pen and they do their best, but you cannot expect a tin plate age to produce a golden age literature. Shakespeare was above all things a triumph of sound education, and the most important thing we know about him is that the headmaster of the Stratford grammar school that he attended received exactly double the salary paid to the then headmaster of Eton. American civilization will not begin to make rapid strides until Americans—not the million dollars a year men only but the ten thousand dollars a year men too—commence to spend a proportion of their money and of their money making time to the acquirement of financially useless knowlege, the exercise of taste and the creation and preservation of that imponderable but unmistakeable thing that we call atmosphere. Not long since while travelling in Canada I asked a young artist friend who had dashed down to New York for a few days what he thought of it. " Well," he said, after a moment's thought, " it's like living inside a gigantic cash register." That one atmosphere of the cash register threatens to envelop the whole United States displacing all that is left of the old atmospheres, the " '49 " atmosphere that still lingers in San Francisco, the Creole atmosphere of New Orleans, the almost forgotten atmospheres of old Virginia, of cultured Boston and Quaker Philadelphia and its picture galleries, the atmosphere of the lumber camp and the range. Attempts to preserve artificially these old atmospheres either in actual life or in books and moving pictures must sooner or later become ridiculous. Is the United States of the future then to have no other than that of the cash register opening and shutting to the neurotic crash and whoop of the jazz band ?

One can hardly turn from this subject without a word about the place of the American woman in American civilization. Apparently she bulks large in what the nation has of intellectual life but only apparently. The American club woman has heard Masfield and Arnold Bennett lecture, she reads Yeats and Galsworthy and is aware of Anatole France. She has nothing else to do while her husband is away at business, for if she does have children she exercises very little control over

them. How little it sinks in, how unmellow-
ed she is by all she reads and hears—
and to be mellowed is the prime object
of the pursuit of culture—can be judged
from her narrowness of outlook, her
hardness of manner and often enough
from her appearance, but most of all
from her utterly negligible contribution
to knowledge, to literature or to the
arts. To take a single example, the
American women's output of poetry,
fiction and ephemeral literature is not
one-fifth in proportion to the total output
of that of the English woman.

The truth is that woman, though she
has always been the great stimulator of
civilization has never been a creator of
it and the American woman does not
in this respect differ from her sisters.
She does differ in this respect that she
has the appearance of being the prime
repository of American culture on the
one hand, while on the other remaining
so excessively female that she has acquired
none of the fine qualities of observation,
detachment and humour that distinguish
the American man. His mistake is
that in his anxiety to be let alone to make
money he allows her to dominate (in
conjunction with the cranks, fanatics
and other "she-men" with which the
States are plentifully provided) situations

that men should and elsewhere do control. This tends to retrogression and will disappear only when the American man broadens his outlook beyond the edge of his counter and his desk.

V

CONCLUSION.

Can we conjure up, from what we know of the United States of to-day, a composite vision of the United States of say a hundred years hence? Let us attempt it, with the usual but important reservation— " if nothing very unexpected happens in the meanwhile." We see the whole of the North American continent from the Arctic Circle to the Mexican Boundary under one flag, a single economic unit all parts of which enjoy the same material civilization and to a great extent the same intellectual civilization. The population of two hundred million odd will be distributed much as it is now save that the Pacific Coast will have gained greatly at the expense of the Atlantic Coast and both will draw still more heavily from the Central plains where the farms will increase steadily in size as the years go on and the work now done by men and women be done more and more by machinery. On the other hand the inevitable slowing up of industrial expansion will have given new vigour to the now almost moribund agricultural life of the New England States, while the doubling of the population combined with the diminishing per acre yield of the older plantations will have brought a great amount of new acreage under cotton and tobacco.

The fruit orchards of the Pacific slope will have undergone a like expansion. The crop however will be for domestic consumption only as American fresh and canned fruit will have been driven from the foreign markets by South African and Australian produce. In the Corn Belt and elsewhere the American will continue to feed and ship the world's pork and bacon, lard and hams, but there will be no great increase of acreage under the plough in the wheat areas. North America will still be well able to produce a vast amount of wheat surplus to domestic requirements but the sale of it will have been organized and Europe will get her bare needs at the top price that can be squeezed out of her. That need will be diminished by the tariff stimulation of wheat growing in Great Britain and Ireland and by the rehabilitation of Russia. On what Russia does depends the future of American wheat. If Russia exercises no organized control over her wheat production but merely produces abundantly and throws her product on the market for what it will fetch North America will have to do the same thing. There will still be a fair profit in wheat but not enough to send new farmers and farm labourers in their thousands to brave the rigours of Alberta and Saskatchewan winters.

There is no real evidence that in the next hundred years the American cotton exporters will be seriously threatened by African or other competition, but it is quite likely that United Kingdom tobacco, protected by heavy duties and dried by new artificial processes, will have cut heavily into the American tobacco trade. I say "United Kingdom" because a reunion, economic and to some extent political, of Ireland with Great Britain must be counted upon. The nexus will be the British tariff on dairy products and cattle which will restore to Ireland the trade in these foodstuffs that Canada is now rapidly taking from her. The future of American petroleum is uncertain. The supply will still be adequate to all probable demands a hundred years hence, but whether the demand will continue or whether some new scientific discovery, for example the wireless transmission of power, will discount it, can only be guessed at.

With his vast and ever increasing and assiduously protected domestic market

at his back the American exporter will
have such an immense advantage over all
competitors in open or partially protected
markets that he will force tariffs and
prices up all over the world. In the open
markets he will be better able to cut
prices than his competitors and so maintain a steady margin of exports over
imports. The value of the wealth thus
accumulated is problematic. Only two
things can be done with it : it can be
lent or spent. To lend it to Europe and
add interest to principle and lend that and
so on may be good for Europe, but it
will do America no good. Wealth is
purchasing power. Will America be able
to go on purchasing to the full extent of
its power or will a large proportion of
it have to be written off ? The things
America purchases in the way of trade
are limited in number and their consumption is limited in extent. The
purchasable, luxuries that could be bought
in unlimited quantities are only for sale
in small quantities. If every old picture
and object d'art sold in Europe in the
next twenty-five years went to America
the bill would not make an appreciable
dent in America's surplus wealth. It is
really up to Europe to devise some
scientific and universal method of sizing
America's pile and charging accordingly
when America comes abroad. America

[85]

will be relieved of some of the blood with which it is bloated and will feel relieved. Europe will likewise be relieved to feel the life-giving stream coursing again through her emaciated financial veins.

The real source of America's top-heavy wealth is not export trade but the immense rise in land and other values. Within the last fifty years or so areas in the Middle West two or three times as big as England have risen in mortgagable value from nothing to three or four hundred dollars an acre. Often the land is worth the enhanced value, not merely because that is what it will fetch, but because of what it will produce in the way of revenue. But much of America's values are inflated, and in these cases America is working a wealth factory overtime when the European hardly has his in operation at all. Take the case of a Los Angeles corner lot, some of which are valued for mortgage purposes at prices a great deal higher than a site in Piccadilly or Cornhill would fetch. Theoretically the price of the Los Angeles lot is based on its productive value as the site of a big store or office building. Actually its value is less because at the time it receives its high valuation it is one of several such lots and it is not possible that the department store or office building in question will be built on all of them. In this way the American by boosting prices enhance, the national wealth. With that wealth he boosts prices again and so acquires more wealth. The process can be increased indefinitely without anybody being a loaf of bread the better for it. Actually the property owners are the better for it because they can increase the value of property quicker than the worker can increase the value of his services or the farmer can increase the value of his grain and stock. That state of things will have disappeared long before our hundred years is up because the farmer is already beginning to organize to keep food prices up. Once all three sources of wealth, property, labour and food have become equally responsive to the booster's touch there will no longer be any point in boosting except to get more money to lend to Europe. And even Europe will not borrow indefinitely.

As the standard of living is steadily rising in America a hundred years hence will find American industrial production about two and a half times what it is to-day. Concentration in the bigger cities is already the rule and we shall have a New York with ten million people, Chicago with five, Philadelphia with three, Detroit and Los Angeles with three or four million apiece and a dozen cities with a million or more apiece.

Life in these great cities will be enormously congested. The total absence of servants will drive all but the artisan class into flats and apartment houses equipped with the latest heating, air cleaning, dust removing appliances and restaurants in which or from which all meals will be served. Milk and vegetables will be obtainable fresh, but eggs, poultry, meat and fruit that have not been in cold storage will be unobtainable. In many States it is already unlawful to expose meat for sale except in a refrigerated glass case! In a hundred years' time, however, the American will have become dyspepsia-proof. It seems likely that the unnatural toughness of his intestines will have set an indelible mark on his features if not on his mind also.

It seems inevitable that long before the hundred years are up the motor car will be the universal method of transportation, and the street car—an intolerable nuisance in a crowded thoroughfare—will be scrapped or driven underground. Vast expenditure, on public highways, state and national, will be made, and it will be possible to traverse North America from coast to coast by a dozen routes without leaving the paved road. One result of this will be that certain parts of the continent, the woods of Ontario, for example, and the beaches of Florida and

California, will become the holiday resorts, not of the wealthy few only, but of the artisan and his family with the antiquated Ford car. As in Britain this immense motor travel will hit the railroads but by that time they will be at the peak of their collars to move all the freight they are required to handle. Their rail mileage however will not increase materially in the next hundred years.

Assuming that the United States closes the door in the face of the European immigrant in the next twenty-five years, as is inevitable, a hundred years from now will find every American with three generations of American born ancestors behind him or her on both sides. This will mean an American almost entirely divorced from the racial passions and national prejudices that now inflame a large number of American citizens. American Irish Republicans will not waylay visiting Irish statesmen with eggs. Anti-Fascists will not greet the arrival of Italian Fascist representatives with pistols. The Arion Club and the Turnverein will no longer act as generating stations of love for the Fatherland and hatred of its enemies. American statesmen-lawyers visiting Westminster will not refer to themselves " sitting at the old home fireside " because American institutions will long have lost all trace of their

British origin. Divested of international
ties the North Americans as a race are
likely to be both aggressive and touchy.
Intensive commercialism will make them
the former and the business of becoming
indigestion-proof will make them the
latter. Whether either quality will embroil
them with their neighbours we cannot
say. International politics is the one
subject on which the speculator has no
present material to work on.

The fusion of all the racial ores in the
American melting pot will not materially
affect the development of American
character which is due to be moulded in
the future by environment and by movement in directions already well defined.
Environment will have a much greater
influence in the next hundred years when
the population will be more or less stationary than in the last hundred years in
which it has been mobile and fluid.
The West being younger will move faster.
California will become the centre of
whatever essentially American intellectual
civilization is developed leaving Massachusetts looking Eastward and mumbling
over the dry bones of its former Americo-
European achievements. The man on
whom it does not snow will still be worth
little as an achiever but California,
rich, sunny, untramelled by history,
unencumbered with tradition, will play

Macaenas to the industrious Northerners and Easterners who come to her with gifts of art and literature, new aesthetic values and the ability to create new and more splendid imaginings. The one really enormous factor that is going to change the surface of American life in the next few decades is that the American is going to learn that it is better and easier to enjoy a little money than to turn a lot of money into more money still. The lesson will be learned first in the West. It may be urged that New York has already learned it. That is not so. New York is a vast cash register. It toils night and day to amuse—and charges accordingly. It is a circus where the audience laugh and the clowns sweat. If the New Yorker does decide to take life easy he nips across and takes it easy in Paris.

It will be well for the United States if the West becomes the nodal point of its intellectual life for the West is sunny and the industrial machine with all the squalor and dirt that follows in its train has never seared its soul. At the present time however the centres of American emotionalism are neither the hectic superficial East nor the sunny, easy money West but the central States. These have bred and will continue to breed most of America's trouble exactly as the great

Central European and Asiatic plains have bred trouble for Western Europe and the Far East. The sea is the great civilizer, the mighty breeder of sanity. The man of steppes and prairies, frozen and roasted by turns has demons gnawing at his vitals. He is the world's crank. Most of America's existing writers, preachers, politicians, and agitators hail from the central plains. So do most of America's cranks, fanatics, revolutionaries, uplifters, patriots and other well meaning trouble-makers. Such people are the destroyers not the upbuilders of intellectual civilizations. To-day they bulk large in the States and it seems that they are destined to have a good innings. Working on the money cravings of the commercial community on the one hand and the political ambitions of such as prefer to live by their tongues or their wits, they are tying the American people up in a coccoon of self-wound inhibitions. Fundamentalism will follow Prohibition. There is no limit to what laws of a similar character may thereafter be passed provided they meet the condition that they facilitate money making.

Salvation will come through the business man's desire to abolish the politician who certainly does not facilitate business. The quadrennial Presidential election costs the United States far more every four years that Prohibition will ever save. The struggle to get rid of the politician will be spectacular but decisive. He will be replaced by the competitively selected life appointee responsible to his non-political Departmental chief. Only the highest offices of state will remain elective. These will no longer carry any patronage with them and as Americans attach no dignity to their public offices and very little salary they will not be coveted by any but mediocre men.

The politician being abolished the cranks and fanatics will have nobody through whom to work. They will work the Referendum and Initiative for all they are worth but the American voter though he lets his politicians enslave him while he gets on with his business will not enslave himself by actively putting a cross on a ballot paper and posting it when he can simply drop it in the Waste Paper basket. Once free of the cranks the American citizen who is for the most part a healthy-minded animal with detachment and a sense of proportion will begin to progress.

He will presumably become more law abiding though here again things in the United States are destined to become worse before they are better. Lawlessness is due to having laws that the public hold in contempt and law enforces subject to political influences and public caprice. In the next fifty years Americans will go on balling themselves up in a still greater tangle of foolish inhibitions and the criminal will continue to defy the law with increasing impunity and incur decreasing disapproval from his fellows. Then as the politicians and cranks disappear, as the machinery of law enforcement is taken out of politics and the freak legislator passes away the unwanted and needlessly restrictive laws and ordinances will pass from the statute books and the needed laws that remain will inspire real respect.

Will the Americans of a hundred years hence have any intellect ? They will have brains, of course, lots of them, business brains and social brains, all the sorts of brains that stimulate immediate action or are called into use by the immediate need of action. Of reflective and analytical brains, of philosophical and imaginative brains and of such brains as are required for the sifting and storing and production at need of knowledge, they will, if they proceed along the road they are now taking, have none at all. A small intellectual class will subsist, subject ever to the temptation to popularize their intellectual attainments in return for a larger share of the good things of life. This class is already absurdly small in comparison with the wealth, numbers and educational facilities of the American people. As the present tendency to superficiality increases, as the vigour of the race is divided more exclusively between money getting and pleasure getting and all life is measured in terms of the pay envelope and the dance floor, that part of the American brain that should be devoted to the acquisition of knowledge, the appreciation of beauty and the exercise of wisdom will atrophy.

When European civilizations reach this unhappy stage as they have done time and again the barbarians have always rushed in and at one blow completed the extinction of the brainless and set to germinating the seed of new and more vigorous cultures. There are no barbarians ready to rush in and submerge the American counting house and lobster palace " in one red burial blent." Moreover the European civilizations that have gone under from time to time were suffering from physical and mental lassitude. America has not even reached the zenith of her potential vigour. It is merely being applied exclusively to material and not at all to spiritual and intellectual things. It is becoming a gigantic Babbitt warren, minus the useful habit of proliferation. Everyone waxes fat and skips in the bright moonshine.

Why not? As a philosophy of life not a serious argument can be advanced against it. Austerity commends itself only to those who have not the wherewithal to be hedonists. High thinking is of value only to those who have to be content with plain living. You may say that the American, divided between "easy money" —for the American has only to be industrious to make money—and elemental enjoyment is not at all attractive to the European who has been taught—mostly by adversity—to regard work as a nuisance and money as valuable only for the interests it allows men to pursue. It is not the American's business to mould himself nearer to the European's desire and there is not the least likelihood that in the next hundred years he will have done so. It is more likely to be the other way about. Europe is moving in the same direction as America. The only difference is that America moves faster and has a long start.

Foreign Travelers in America
1810–1935

AN ARNO PRESS COLLECTION

Archer, William. **America To-Day:** Observations and Reflections. 1899.

Belloc, Hilaire. **The Contrast.** 1924.

[Boardman, James]. **America, and the Americans.** By a Citizen of the World. 1833.

Bose, Sudhindra. **Fifteen Years in America.** 1920.

Bretherton, C. H. **Midas, Or, The United States and the Future.** 1926.

Bridge, James Howard (Harold Brydges). **Uncle Sam at Home.** 1888.

Brown, Elijah (Alan Raleigh). **The Real America.** 1913.

Combe, George. **Notes on the United States Of North America During a Phrenological Visit in 1838-9-40.** 1841. 2 volumes in one.

D'Estournelles de Constant, Paul H. B. **America and Her Problems.** 1915.

Duhamel, Georges. **America the Menace:** Scenes from the Life of the Future. Translated by Charles Miner Thompson. 1931.

Feiler, Arthur. **America Seen Through German Eyes.** Translated by Margaret Leland Goldsmith. 1928.

Fidler, Isaac. **Observations on Professions, Literature, Manners, and Emigration, in the United States and Canada, Made During a Residence There in 1832.** 1833.

Fitzgerald, William G. (Ignatius Phayre). **Can America Last?** A Survey of the Emigrant Empire from the Wilderness to World-Power Together With Its Claim to "Sovereignty" in the Western Hemisphere from Pole to Pole. 1933.

Gibbs, Philip. **People of Destiny:** Americans As I Saw Them at Home and Abroad. 1920.

Graham, Stephen. **With Poor Immigrants to America.** 1914.

Griffin, Lepel Henry. **The Great Republic.** 1884.

Hall, Basil. **Travels in North America in the Years 1827 and 1828.** 1829. 3 volumes in one.

Hannay, James Owen (George A. Birmingham). **From Dublin to Chicago:** Some Notes on a Tour in America. 1914.

Hardy, Mary (McDowell) Duffus. **Through Cities and Prairie Lands:** Sketches of an American Tour. 1881.

Holmes, Isaac. **An Account of the United States of America,** Derived from Actual Observation, During a Residence of Four Years in That République, Including Original Communications. [1823].

Ilf, Ilya and Eugene Petrov. **Little Golden America:** Two Famous Soviet Humorists Survey These United States. Translated by Charles Malamuth. 1937.

Kerr, Lennox. **Back Door Guest.** 1930.

Kipling, Rudyard. **American Notes.** 1899.

Leng, John. **America in 1876:** Pencillings During a Tour in the Centennial Year, With a Chapter on the Aspects of American Life. 1877.

Longworth, Maria Theresa (Yelverton). **Teresina in America.** 1875. 2 volumes in one.

Low, A[lfred] Maurice. **America at Home.** [1908].

Marshall, W[alter] G[ore]. **Through America:** Or, Nine Months in the United States. 1881.

Mitchell, Ronald Elwy. **America:** A Practical Handbook. 1935.

Moehring, Eugene P. **Urban America and the Foreign Traveler, 1815-1855.** With Selected Documents on 19th-Century American Cities. 1974.

Muir, Ramsay. **America the Golden:** An Englishman's Notes and Comparisons. 1927.

Price, M[organ] Philips. **America After Sixty Years:** The Travel Diaries of Two Generations of Englishmen. 1936.

Sala, George Augustus. **America Revisited:** From the Bay of New York to the Gulf of Mexico and from Lake Michigan to the Pacific. 1883. 3rd edition. 2 volumes in one.

Saunders, William. **Through the Light Continent;** Or, the United States in 1877-8. 1879. 2nd edition.

Smith, Frederick [Edwin] (Lord Birkenhead). **My American Visit.** 1918.

Stuart, James. **Three Years in North America.** 1833. 2 volumes in one.

Teeling, William. **American Stew.** 1933.

Vivian, H. Hussey. **Notes of a Tour in America from August 7th to November 17th, 1877.** 1878.

Wagner, Charles. **My Impressions of America.** Translated by Mary Louise Hendee. 1906.

Wells, H. G. **The Future in America:** A Search After Realities. 1906.